This

ILL Condition Report
This item was received in the
Following condition:

Loose pages	☐
Torn cover/pages	☐
Missing pages	☐
Loose/broken spine	☒
Water/stain damaged	☐
Writing in book	☐
Chewed	☐
Other	5/17/22

SALT LAKE
COUNTY
LIBRARY
SERVICES

off
Intern   ub.

Joined on:

With special thanks to George, William, Ella and Eve

First published in the UK in 2014 by

Ivy Press

210 High Street

Lewes

East Sussex BN7 2NS

United Kingdom

www.ivypress.co.uk

ISBN: 978-1-78240-105-6

This book was conceived, designed & produced by

Ivy Press

CREATIVE DIRECTOR	Peter Bridgewater
MANAGING EDITOR	Hazel Songhurst
COMMISSIONING EDITOR	Georgia Amson-Bradshaw
PROJECT EDITOR	Georgia Amson-Bradshaw
ART DIRECTOR	Kim Hankinson
DESIGNERS	Joanna Clinch and Kim Hankinson
ILLUSTRATOR	David Broadbent

Text by Bernadette Russell

Printed in China

Distributed worldwide (except North America) by Thames & Hudson Ltd.
181A High Holborn, London WC1V 7QX, United Kingdom

Colour origination by Ivy Press Reprographics

10 9 8 7 6 5 4 3 2

DO NICE
BE KIND
SPREAD HAPPY

BY
BERNADETTE RUSSELL

Acts of
Kindness
for Kids

IVY KIDS

CONGRATULATIONS!

Now you have this incredible book, you automatically gain membership of the worldwide 'Kindness club' - a secret society of undercover agents with a common purpose: to spread happiness, smiles, magic and a bit of mischief throughout our world by committing acts of ninja niceness.

And do you know the most powerful thing about your acts of kindness? Kind acts make people happy, and happy people are nice to others, so the movement grows and grows.

WELL DONE!

BRAVO!

Your Mission:

★ To use the suggestions in this book to spread the power of kindness in your neighbourhood.

★ To recruit new members to the Kindness Club whenever possible.

★ To solemnly vow to 1. uphold the duties of a happiness hero, 2. commit to the kindness cause, and 3. have as much fun as possible whilst doing it.

★ To keep a record of where and when you completed your kindness deeds by using the tick boxes provided in this book. (This way you get a kindness diary to keep and to help you remember how AMAZING you are).

★ To cut out the badges on the inside of the cover, tape safety pins on the backs of them, and wear them with PRIDE.

GOOD LUCK WITH YOUR MISSIONS, AND REMEMBER TO RECORD YOUR KINDNESS ADVENTURES BY TICKING THE CHECK BOX ON EACH PAGE AND MAKING A NOTE ABOUT HOW THEY WENT.

WOOF!

Dogs are great company. Why not make yourself a 'Hound Hero' by offering to take your neighbour's pet for a walk? You could even do it regularly: great for the dog (who gets a walk), the neighbour (who gets a rest), and you (who gets a dog for company and some exercise)! For bonus points you could teach the dog a trick, such as how to high-five, to surprise the owner when you and Dog return home.

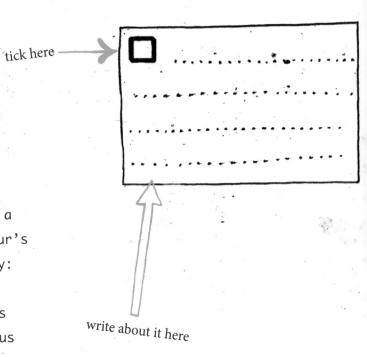

tick here →

write about it here

HAPPY UNBIRTHDAY

Uh-oh! You forgot Auntie Natalie/Cousin Asif/your best friend Joe's birthday.

You feel bad. There's no excuse. Oh well, there's always next year... hold on a minute... why not surprise them with a Happy Unbirthday card?

Smile Collection Mission

Spend one whole day saying hello and smiling at absolutely everyone you see.

Don't worry if they look a bit surprised, or think you might be a bit of a loony. Every time you get a smile or a hello back, count them up and do a tally at the end of the day.

You could try a smile competition with a friend. Your mission: to beat each other at the number of smiles and hellos you manage to receive in one day.

PASS THE PARCEL

You know those books that you just can't stop reading? The ones where you're sorry when it ends, because it's been so good you'd like it to go on forever??

Why not pass that book on to a random stranger?
write a note on the inside cover saying why you liked it,
and that you hope they like it just as much.

Suggest that when they have finished
reading they leave it in a public space for
another stranger to pick up.

Return to Sender

Write a note starting 'Dear Post Person', then go on to thank them in general 'for all the letters' and maybe in particular for something (such as 'for the birthday card from my Grandad').

Perhaps you could add some sweets as a little treat for them to keep their energy up on their rounds.

Without postmen and women we'd get fewer birthday cards and gifts, that's for sure. Next time you see her or him coming to the door – deliver your own post right back to them!

REVERSE ROBBING

Think of someone who really deserves a treat. What do they like? A certain chocolate bar or magazine? New pens? A postcard with a funny message?

Once you've decided on a 'victim' and what they might like, sneak something into their bag or coat pocket. Make sure they don't notice you doing it. Leave a note with it simply saying 'SURPRISE! You've been reverse-robbed!' Keep it anonymous and see if you can keep a straight face when they tell you about it.

GETTING WARMER

Here at Kindness HQ, we like to wear three sweaters, four pairs of socks and two hats. And that's just in the summer. You should see us in the winter!

Only joking of course, but it does get pretty chilly – can you imagine what it would be like to go without a coat to put on? Or to sleep out in the cold all night?

We all have clothes that we don't wear: why not ask your friends/neighbours/ relatives to donate one coat that they no longer use, and then give them to a homeless charity...

...But before you do, put a note inside the pocket of each coat as a surprise for the person who gets it.

Something like;

'This coat belonged to my friend Ryan. His arms got too long for it; I hope it looks better on you, and keeps you warm.'

or

'This jacket was my mum's. My Dad got it for her for Christmas, but now it's a present for you.'

These notes will make the coat an even better gift.

What a load of trash

You will need:
- a pair of old gloves
- something to take 'before and after' pics with.

Give the street cleaner a hand:
take a 'before' picture of a particularly messy area, then
spend half an hour
clearing all the trash away
(keep your gloves on -some of the trash can get pretty DISGUSTING).
Then take
an 'after' picture. You can be in the picture so everyone knows it was you, or you might prefer to remain mysterious...

HUG THROUGH THE POST

Get someone to draw around your outstretched arms on the plain side of a piece of lining paper, wallpaper or wrapping paper (you need something long enough to stretch your arms out on).

Carefully cut around the shape that they have drawn.

Write your name on the back, and send it to someone you like but don't see very often with a message:

'a BIG hug from ******'

New Kid In Town

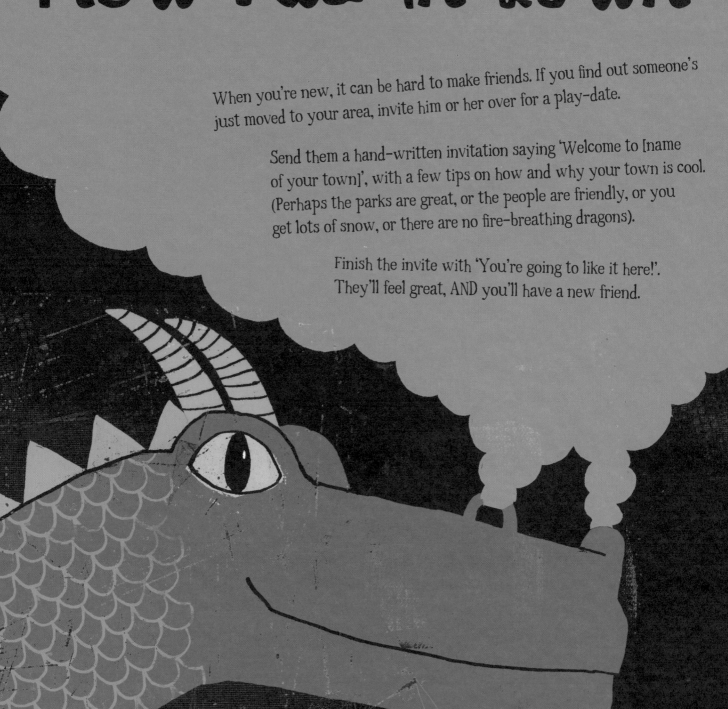

When you're new, it can be hard to make friends. If you find out someone's just moved to your area, invite him or her over for a play-date.

Send them a hand-written invitation saying 'Welcome to [name of your town]', with a few tips on how and why your town is cool. (Perhaps the parks are great, or the people are friendly, or you get lots of snow, or there are no fire-breathing dragons).

Finish the invite with 'You're going to like it here!'. They'll feel great, AND you'll have a new friend.

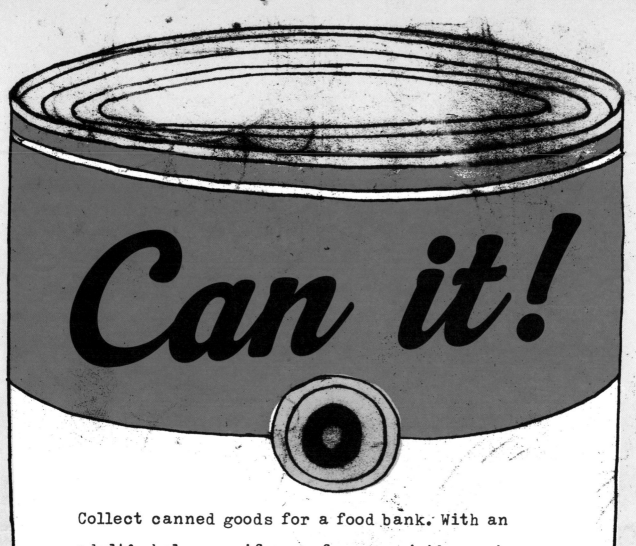

Can it!

Collect canned goods for a food bank. With an adult's help, see if any of your neighbours have anything to spare. This way you'll get a chance to meet them all, too (I did this and now my neighbours bring round cake for me whenever they've made one, which is a Good Thing). Once you've collected all the food, take it to the food bank with a note saying 'From all of us on [your street name]'.

COMPLIMENT SLIP

In the Olden Days before emails, offices used to give out pieces of paper called compliment slips. My mum said it always disappointed her that there was never an actual compliment on them, so let's fix that!

Use strips of scrap paper with some ready prepared compliments such as:

'That is the best hat in town!'

'Your hair has made me happy.'

Carry spares with you so you can write more. Grab the opportunity to make someone's day by handing him or her one.

(If you are feeling extra brave, you could just say it.)

ALL GROWN UP

Are you holding on to loads of toys and books that you had as a baby? You could keep one toy and one book, then be brave and give away all your other baby books and toys to charity or to a children's hospital. The good things about this are, a) you'll feel proud you helped out younger kids, and b) you'll have more room for your cool new stuff.

Be a PORTER for a DAY

Everybody likes to be greeted with a beaming smile, so why not try a bit of 'portering'? You could do this at home, at school, at the library – anywhere you often go. You need a gigantic grin, and maybe a hat or a smart outfit. Surprise people by holding the door open for them. Try saying: 'Good morning Sir/Madam, welcome to [name of your street/school/the building], please come in – I hope you have a very nice day.' Do a little old-fashioned bow, and smile.

Why not try greeting people in a few different languages – this is fun and impressive, and it's a good thing to speak as many languages as possible. (I'm aiming for 17 at least. So far I'm on one). Here are some examples to get you started:

SABAH-IL-KHEIR

Arabic

ZAO SHANG HAO

Chinese (Mandarin)

BONJOUR

French

DOBRAYE OOTRA

Russian

SHUBH PRABHAT

Hindi

TIP:
Prevent 'smiler's cramp' by wriggling your face around a bit during the day.

ROOM WITH A VIEW

My sister Kim was complaining that all she could see from her kitchen window was a rusty bucket and some cats fighting. This gave me an idea: to plant something beautiful that, when it grows, will be clearly seen from someone's window. One day they'll look out and a lovely red geranium or yellow sunflower will make their view much better.

Lovely!

SCHOOL REPORT

Write a report for your teacher, with grades.
Make a list of all the ways in which they are excellent.

It could be like this:

Making me laugh: A+
Mr/Miss has made an excellent
effort at being funny all term.

Helping me with maths: A+
Mr/Miss has been patient with me
and with the numbers.

Being kind: A+
Mr/Miss has been very good
at being kind, even in very
noisy circumstances.

**Put it in an official-looking
envelope and give it to them,
or leave it on their desk.**

Graffiti of Kindness

Real graffiti isn't allowed, of course, so first check with an adult if it's ok to use chalk in your neighbourhood. If it is, chalk messages on the pavement or on the path in the park, (like 'Hope you have a great day', or 'Good morning. I hope the sun's shining and that this message makes you smile. Love from the Park Pixie'). If chalk is not allowed, no problem! Write the message using pebbles or leaves. This will take longer but looks beautiful. You'll bring a bit of mystery to your neighbourhood – 'Who is this Park Pixie?', they will ask.

ROUND OF APPLAUSE

Look after your bus driver. Say hello when you get on the bus and thank you when you get off. I do this for my bus driver, and he often treats us to a song. Luckily for me he has a great voice. If you get the school bus, get everyone to do a great big round of applause for the driver at the end of term, plus a few HIP HIP HOORAYS! Bus drivers keep us safe and get us to where we need to go. They deserve a bit of praise.

SHOWTIME!

It's expensive to go out - if you can sing, dance or play an instrument you could treat someone to his or her very own show! Rehearse on your own or with friends or siblings.

Write a programme and give your show a title. Surprise a neighbour or relative by entertaining them - it could be on their doorstep, in their kitchen, or by invitation to your house.

If it goes down well (I bet it will) you could repeat your show for others. It could be the start of something big. (I'm thinking YouTube hit!)

Sticky Notes

Grab a stack of sticky notes and get scribbling. Write messages such as:

Don't work too hard!

Today is definitely going to be great.

EVERYBODY SAYS YOU ARE AWESOME

Stick them in places that people might need cheering up.

You could ask an adult to take them into a workplace and put them on people's desks for you.

Be crafty!

It's so annoying to lose your place in a book. The solution: bookmarks! They're fun and easy to make out of recycled stuff, and a great thing to give away.

You will need:
. . . .

card
(e.g. an old cereal box)
scissors
glue
stuff to decorate your bookmark
(whatever you like: pictures from old
magazines, feathers, flowers, leaves,
glitter, sequins, paint… anything goes)

Your bookmark should be longer than a regular-sized book. Measure your card against a book you have at home, then carefully cut a strip.

The person you give it to will see this bookmark every time they go back to their book, so you may want to leave a message.

It could be something like 'No act of kindness, however small, is ever wasted', or 'Reading this is definitely going to make you smarter'. If you're feeling arty you could draw pictures or patterns.

Then choose someone to give it to.

Easy.

A GOOD MORNING

Give your parent(s), grandparent(s) or guardian(s) a great start to the day by leaving them a note telling them why they are special to you.

It could be something like 'Mum, you tell good stories and make nice dinner.' Put it somewhere where it will surprise them first thing in the morning.

Some ideas for good hiding places: in the fridge, by the kettle, on the back of the front door, on the car seat, on the bathroom mirror, under the cat.

(P.S. Not that last one. Cats aren't good hiding places really. I was being silly).

Music makes everyone happy! Think of someone you know who needs cheering up, and make them a playlist of songs to make them smile. Put all the songs on a CD and make a cover for it saying 'songs that remind me of you.' Spend time

Songs for Somebody

on it so it's not just songs you like, but songs with their name in, or about things they like. The cover of the CD could be a photo of you and them together.

Goody Bag

There are loads of things that we take for granted that can be tougher to get if you're homeless.

Make a goody bag containing stuff like a toothbrush and some toothpaste, deodorant, spare socks, gloves in winter, plus anything else you think might be nice or useful. You could also include a card saying 'I hope things get easier for you'.

Groceries are good, too, if you have spare stuff in your house. But the best thing of all is being friendly, so if you give it to someone on the street make sure you also give them a smile.

Picture this.

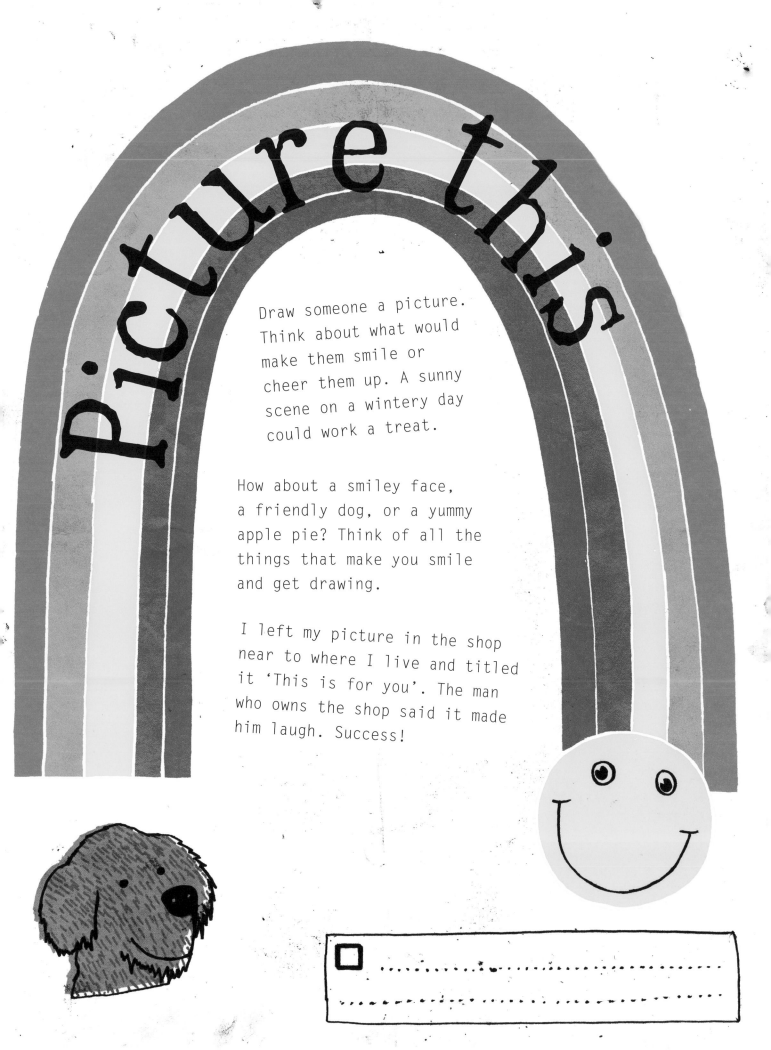

Draw someone a picture. Think about what would make them smile or cheer them up. A sunny scene on a wintery day could work a treat.

How about a smiley face, a friendly dog, or a yummy apple pie? Think of all the things that make you smile and get drawing.

I left my picture in the shop near to where I live and titled it 'This is for you'. The man who owns the shop said it made him laugh. Success!

CHANGE THE WORLD

Recycle an old jar, and start a loose change collection at home. Ask everyone to drop in whatever change they can spare. When the jar is full, donate the money to your favourite organisation or charity. Everyone at home could take it in turns to nominate a good cause of his or her own. Keep a tally of how much you raise each time the jar is full, and watch it all add up!

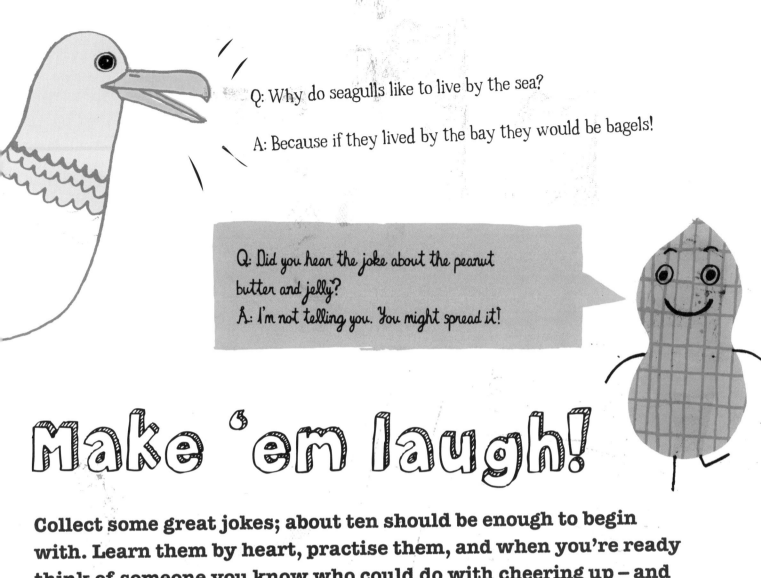

Q: Why do seagulls like to live by the sea?

A: Because if they lived by the bay they would be bagels!

Q: Did you hear the joke about the peanut butter and jelly?
A: I'm not telling you. You might spread it!

Make 'em laugh!

Collect some great jokes; about ten should be enough to begin with. Learn them by heart, practise them, and when you're ready think of someone you know who could do with cheering up – and do a little comedy show for them. Here are some of my friend William's favourite jokes:

Q: What do you call a dinosaur with no eyes?

A: Doyouthinkysaurus

PEN PALS

Make friends with someone in a different part of the world. Ask at school for contacts, or get your parents or guardians to ask their friends if they know of anyone your age in another country who would like a pen pal.

Once you have a pen pal you could send them an email but handwritten letters are even better. I get excited whenever I get something through the post, as it feels like it's my birthday, even when it isn't!

You could send them:

* DRAWINGS OF YOU AND YOUR FAMILY, YOUR HOME AND YOUR FRIENDS

* PHOTOS OF THE PLACE WHERE YOU LIVE, AND YOUR FAVOURITE DINNER (SERIOUSLY, THIS SOUNDS A BIT BONKERS BUT ALL OVER THE WORLD PEOPLE EAT WEIRD AND WONDERFUL STUFF)

* INFORMATION ABOUT YOUR LIFE (YOUR SCHOOL, YOUR HOBBIES AND WHAT YOU DO IN YOUR SPARE TIME). ASK LOTS OF QUESTIONS TO FIND OUT ABOUT THEM

TELL THEM ABOUT THE KINDNESS CLUB AND GET THEM TO JOIN IN AND START SPREADING KINDNESS AROUND THE WORLD! A GREAT WEBSITE FOR FINDING A PEN PAL IS WWW.STUDENTSOFTHEWORLD.INFO

Letters of kindness

Put together a letter-writing kit (with pens, envelopes, paper and stamps), and give it to a retirement home.

This is great way to help seniors keep in touch with friends and family who live a long way away.

You could even offer to post their letters for them, too! I made a 'mail bag' out of an old pillowcase and delivered a bunch of letters from the old folks' home. I got a lot of thanks and two cookies – yum!

PASS IT ON

Teach someone something you already know how to do – like how to ride a bike, or how to swim, read, draw, write stories, or play basketball or the recorder. Start by writing a list of all the cool things you can do, and ask your friends or family if they'd like to learn any of them too.

Idea: skill swap! If you're really great at painting and your friend George is brilliant at swimming, you could help each other learn. Everyone's a winner!

It always amazes me when I see a flower grow from an itsy-bitsy seed, as if by magic. A packet of seeds is super cheap and makes a great gift. Or grow some flowers from seeds yourself in a garden or window box, and give them away when they're grown. When you give your gift you can proudly say, 'I grew this myself!'

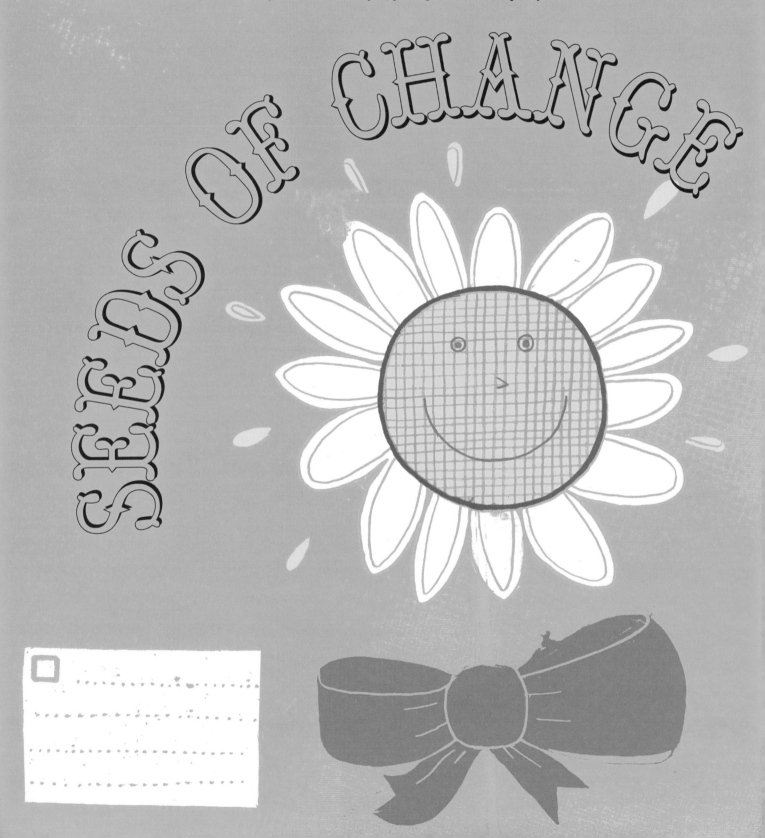

SEEDS OF CHANGE

Go-Cart

Grocery shopping can be a bit boring.

Often when you've finished the actual shopping part and loaded the bags into the car, all you want to do is go home and eat some of the yummy stuff you've just bought. Save a shopper one last job by offering to return their shopping trolley to the trolley park. If it's the kind where you get a coin back, run back over and return it to them.

(If you are lucky enough to get to keep it, you COULD donate it to charity as a Double Dose of Good Deed.)

KNOCK DOWN GINGER

This is a very old tradition, and no one can remember why it's called 'ginger' — even my red-haired friend Siobhan who is pretty old herself. It's a mystery. Anyhow, it's good fun and simple: leave a small gift on the front porch for a friend or neighbour, knock on the door, and run away! If you're brave you could spy from a distance, and see their surprise.

TIP: You could leave some cookies you baked, or a poem you wrote, or anything else nice. Gift wrapping it is good fun and makes it more exciting for them.

say CHEESE

I often see people trying to take photographs of themselves and their friends around town. You could offer to take a picture of a group, family, or couple who have a camera and are capturing the moment.

If you think they're visitors you could say, 'Welcome to [name of your town]'. They'll think your town has the friendliest people EVER!

Adverts for HAPPINESS

Take out an advert in the window of your local newsagent's to spread the message of kindness! Normally it's very cheap to place a card in a newsagent's window and your newsagent may even do it for free once they know what it's for.

Have a look at the cards already in the window: they often say stuff like 'Bike for Sale' or 'Room to Let', written in plain black ink. Make sure yours stands out by using bright colours.

Bike For Sale

Room to Let

Make the world
a happier place:
say good morning,
hold open a door,
and help each
other out.

I dare you to
smile at a total
stranger today.
Go on, try it.
(You have a great
smile.)

Be kind. It's
much easier
than being
mean. And
it's more fun.

Join The
Kindness Club
- DO NICE, BE
KIND, SPREAD
HAPPY!

BEST GUEST EVER

After my birthday party last year, my home looked like it had been attacked by a gang of giant ice cream-eating mice who'd thrown cake everywhere. It was a great party but it was a tough clean up; no one looks forward to that part. Next time you go to a party, why not stay behind and help your host clear up? Put rubbish in the bin, pick stuff up, and put everything back where it should be. If you do this you're pretty much guaranteed to be invited to every party ever.

We all know how boring
it can be just waiting. Why not collect
up any old magazines or comics you have and
drop them off at hospitals, nursing homes,

and dentist's waiting rooms? Your mum and dad
probably have loads they'd be glad to be rid of, so
instead of recycling them or letting them build
up in a huge pile, take them somewhere
they will be appreciated!

☐ ....
....

BE PUSHY*

Give kids free swing pushes in the park. Sometimes small legs have trouble getting going, and as a bonus your arms will get stronger and stronger.

* WARNING: Check that the kids actually want a push first, and that their parents don't mind.

SECOND WARNING: Go gentle, in case you underestimate your own strength and send them hurtling into the sky. (It could be tricky to explain how you managed to push a little kid into outer space.)

Remember: Little kids, little pushes, big fun. You'll be a hero.

Lots of rescue animals are waiting for a home, but they need a lot of love and attention. They also need walks, grooming, cleaning out, feeding and watering. Speak to your parents or guardians about this one — if you reckon you've got what it takes to look after an animal EVERY day and they agree, go for it! I adopted a dog named Lexie and now we both have lots of friends in the park — I talk to mine while she chases hers around.

ADOPT A PET

A Cool Gift

It's been a lovely hot summer here at Kindness HQ, which gave us this great idea: next time you go to get an ice cream or ice lolly to cool you down, buy two!

You could spring a big surprise by giving it straight away to the person behind you in the queue, or you could take it away and deliver it to someone you know who is overheating! A cool kindness for a hot day.

MAKE A WISH

GRANT SOME WISHES! GET SOME GOLD OR SILVER STARS FROM A CRAFT STORE, AND MAKE A SIMPLE CARD BY STICKING THE STAR IN THE MIDDLE AND WRITING:

'MAKE A WISH UPON THIS STAR. SLEEP WITH THIS CARD UNDER YOUR PILLOW AND YOUR WISH MIGHT COME TRUE... LOVE FROM YOUR WISH WIZARD/FAIRY GODMOTHER'.

YOU COULD PLACE IT INSIDE AN ENVELOPE LABELLED 'PLEASE PICK ME UP' AND LEAVE IT SOMEWHERE SOMEONE WILL FIND IT. GOOD PLACES TO LEAVE YOUR WISH: INSIDE A BOOK IN A SHOP OR LIBRARY, ON THE SEAT OF A BUS, BY THE FRONT DOOR OF YOUR HOME.

MAGICAL

Leave a series of clues throughout your house, leading to a great surprise for a family member.

For example: leave a note on your brother's/sister's/dad's door saying, 'Look in the right-hand pocket of your favourite coat'. Then leave another note there saying something like, 'Look in the blue flowery cup in the kitchen cupboard'. Then ANOTHER note there saying, 'Look under the back door mat', and so on.

MYSTERY TOUR

Do as many as you like - you could have them leading all over the house, into the garden, and up and down stairs. Some of them could be harder to find than others (a good one is 'Look inside a sock in your drawer', if they have plenty of socks this will take a while).

In the very last place hide a surprise. This could be a note saying 'BEST DAD EVER', a pretty flower you've picked, a drawing you've done of them, or a little present. You could even hide yourself in the final place and deliver the message personally!

WELCOME HOME

PEOPLE SOMETIMES GET BANNERS WHEN THEY'VE BEEN AWAY FOR AGES, BUT WHY NOT MAKE ONE SAYING 'WELCOME HOME' FOR MUM OR DAD ON A COMPLETELY ORDINARY DAY?

YOU COULD MAKE IT OUT OF A ROLL OF WRAPPING PAPER AND SOME THICK PENS. MAYBE PUT UP SOME BALLOONS, AND HAVE THEIR FAVOURITE DRINK READY.

IF YOU HAVE BROTHERS AND SISTERS TOO, GET THEM TO JOIN IN WHEN YOU SHOUT, 'WELCOME HOME!' AS MUM OR DAD WALKS THROUGH THE DOOR. WARNING: DON'T SHOUT TOO LOUDLY IN CASE IT IS FRIGHTENING AND MAKES THEM RUN AWAY. QUITE LOUD SHOUTING WILL PROBABLY DO IT.

HOLIDAY HELPER

Lots of nursing homes have special events at holiday times: ask if you could help by serving tea or coffee, or donating some prizes for a raffle. Find out what kind of activities they like to do there. If you're feeling daring maybe you could offer to sing a song – something everyone could join in with. I did this and took my ukulele.

SOME SONG IDEAS (FROM MY GRANDAD):

You Are My Sunshine
I'm Forever Blowing Bubbles
Big Rock Candy Mountain
Que Sera, Sera

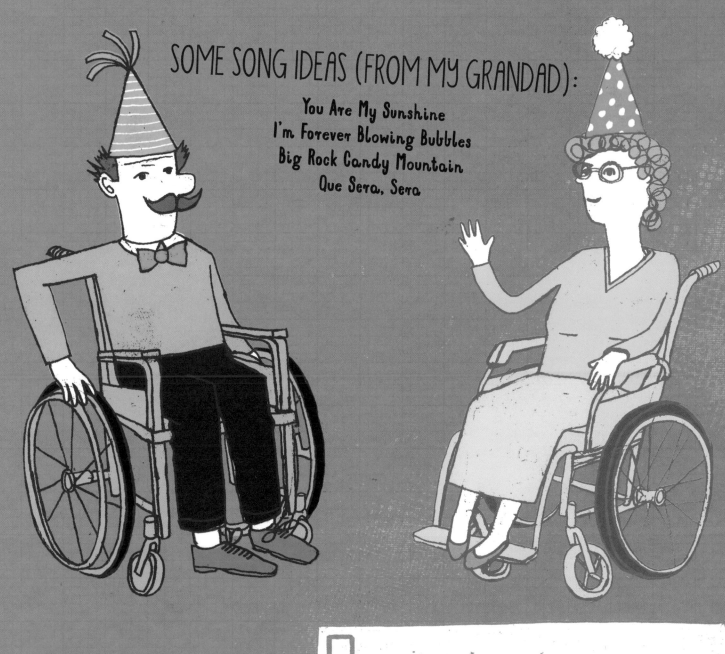

Get Well Soon

Make a handmade card to send to a children's hospital, with an 'I hope you feel better soon' message. Make it colourful and cheerful. You could draw a self-portrait on the inside of the card so that the recipient will know what you look like.

EXTRA:

You could collect unwanted toys from your friends and take them to the hospital too. Hospitals need to be able to clean toys thoroughly, so plastic toys are the best.

NEXT TIME YOU GET SOMETHING FROM A VENDING MACHINE, AND THERE'S A BIT OF MONEY LEFT OVER, LEAVE IT IN THERE. IT MIGHT EVEN BE ENOUGH FOR THE NEXT PERSON TO GET A FREE TREAT. IF YOU SIT NEAR THE VENDING MACHINE, YOU MIGHT SEE THE NEXT PERSON GET THIS NICE SURPRISE, AND SEE THE LOOK ON THEIR FACE. IT'S ALWAYS GREAT TO GET SOMETHING FOR FREE WHEN YOU LEAST EXPECT IT!

kindness for kids

Remember: to your little brothers/sisters/cousins you are cool, just because you're bigger than them. It can sometimes be a bit annoying when they follow you around, but it's a compliment that they want to be with you, so be friendly and don't push them away. Why not recruit them into your niceness adventures? You'll have a ready-made kindness gang to help spread the word!

Jolly Jam

WARNING: Best to do this when the car is STILL, so as not to distract drivers. But you know that, obviously.

When I was in my car last week it seemed like everyone wanted to go home at the same time. My mum and I were stuck in a traffic jam. Luckily I had pens and paper, so I made signs to hold up at the windows for our road-neighbours, who looked very bored. It made them smile and wave! So when you're in a car at a standstill you could make signs (saying 'hello' or 'you're nearly there', with a smiley face drawn on) to hold up at the window.

I call this 'Be Your Own Best Friend Day'. Start as soon as you wake up. Go and look in the mirror and tell yourself how great you are; how you have lovely brown eyes and a nice smile, and so on. Pay yourself lots of compliments. Write a list of all the great things about you, and all the wonderful things in your life, then read it out loud: I promise you this will work like magic, you'll feel great.

Next, make a list of the top ten things you like doing. Put this list somewhere you will be able to see it every day. Make a promise to yourself that every month you'll do each of your favourite things at least once, (as long as those things aren't 'Travel to Mars in a spaceship' or 'Turn into an elephant for a day', as those could be tricky). You'll be much better at being kind to others, if you feel happy because you've been kind to yourself.

Be happy.
Enjoy yourself. You deserve it.
(I say so.)

EMERGENCY

There are actually real-life superheroes living near you. Who am I talking about? Firefighters. It's a dangerous job that requires courage, strength and energy. You could help out with that last part by giving them a box of treats to keep them going on a long shift. Add a thank-you note – tell them how much you appreciate them keeping the neighbourhood safe. If you're lucky you might get to see a fire engine!

SERVICE

CAR WASH

I wrote with my finger 'please wash me' in the mud on my neighbour's car, then I showed him and offered to wash it for him.

He was so surprised he was speechless at first, but once he'd recovered he said, 'Yes, please!'.

On a sunny day, with a bucket of foamy water and a friend, car washing can actually be good fun.

TIP
Try not to wash yourself in the process.

WAITING FOR IT

Next time you're at a coffee shop or restaurant, write something nice about your waitperson on the back of the bill.

Waiting tables can be a tough job with long hours and some tricky customers (not you, of course).

Ask their name, then write down all the things that you think are great about them.

You could draw them a picture with the message 'Don't work too hard.' You'll be the Best Customer Ever.

Lending a hand

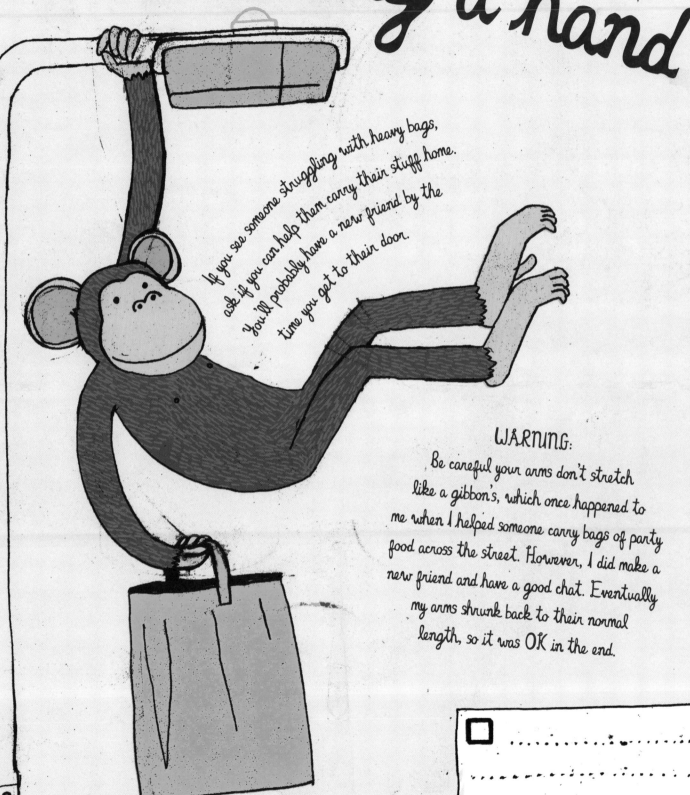

If you see someone struggling with heavy bags, ask if you can help them carry their stuff home. You'll probably have a new friend by the time you get to their door.

WARNING:
Be careful your arms don't stretch like a gibbon's, which once happened to me when I helped someone carry bags of party food across the street. However, I did make a new friend and have a good chat. Eventually my arms shrunk back to their normal length, so it was OK in the end.

Gather a group of friends/ brothers/sisters/cousins. Everybody writes down his or her name on a scrap of paper, folds it so the name can't be seen and puts it in a hat. (If there's no hat around you could use a box, a bucket or a very large pair of hands. You get the idea.)

Have everyone pick out a name. The mission is to do one act of kindness for that person within a week. At the end of the week, the whole group gets together and swaps stories of kindness.

If it goes well, you could make it a regular event.

Hat Trick

Get PACKING

Next time you go to the shop, see if you can find anyone who looks like they could do with some help packing their groceries into their car. They'll be pleased, as this is a boring job to do on your own.

WARNING: Make sure you pick bags you can actually lift. I once tried to help a lady with a bag of potatoes and I fell over.

WINDOW DRESSING

WE HOPE THE BEST

Think how nice it would be if every time someone passed your house they saw something in the window to cheer them up.

Ask your parents or guardians if there are any old pillowcases or sheets or large pieces of paper, such as old wallpaper or wrapping paper, that you could use for the messages. You'll also need paints or pens. Think of a message you'd like to share with the world.

OU HAVE
AY EVER!

Here are some examples of what we've put up in our windows at Kindness HQ:

★ Smile, it's catching!
★ We hope you have the best day ever!
★ Today is going to be excellent - I can tell!

Stick the sign to your window, with the message side facing out. Every passer-by will see it; that's a lot of people, so make sure it's bright and colourful. You could do a different message on the first day of every month, and your home will become famous far and wide for the messages of kindness.

gimme shelter!

Just when you thought it was going to be sunny all day, it starts to rain – and you're going to get soaked to the skin.

Ugh! If you see this happening to someone, offer to shelter him or her under your umbrella. If you have a spare and it's a rainy day, you could leave it outside your house, with a sign saying 'please take me'.

TIP: If you share with anyone a lot taller than you, get them to hold the umbrella. Otherwise your arms will get super-stretched, and they will get neck ache from bending down – a hazard of umbrella-sharing.

I used to struggle with my maths homework until my friend Antje helped me and it all started to make more sense. If you have a subject you find easy and you know someone who is struggling, offer to help. It is easier to learn in pairs, and doing homework is much more fun with someone else. You might have time after the homework to do something fun together, too.

GO MOW

Offer to mow a neighbour's lawn – it's easy, good exercise, plus freshly cut grass smells AMAZING.

Or you could do it as a surprise: my sister Kim and I snuck next door to our neighbour Leo's garden and mowed his lawn while he was out.

Check with an adult first if it's OK to do this for your neighbour (in case they like their grass long, because it's very difficult to put back once it's cut). You will soon gain the reputation of Best Neighbour Ever.

WORLD KINDNESS DAY

Did you know such a day existed? Well, it does! Every year on November 13th people all over the world are celebrating kindness and sharing their stories - now YOU are part of that amazing mission! Let everyone know about World Kindness Day - share what you've been doing and recruit other members to the Kindness Club! You could spend this day saying 'Happy World Kindness Day' to everyone you meet. People will ask what it's all about and you can tell them all about your kindness adventures and future plans.

The Tree of Kindness

Write messages of kindness on ribbons of fabric (I used an old bed sheet torn into strips; ask your parents if they have anything lying around). Every day, write a new message on a strip and tie it to a tree branch.

This could be a tree on the street where you live, or in the park. It will be exciting to watch the messages build up over time! You could encourage other people to join in, by leaving a sign on the trunk of the tree explaining your mission (cover the sign in plastic to guard against bad weather).

If possible, write your messages with a waterproof pen (this is a lot easier than trying to bring the tree inside when it rains, believe me). In a short space of time, the tree will be covered in loveliness and you can enjoy watching people stop to read.

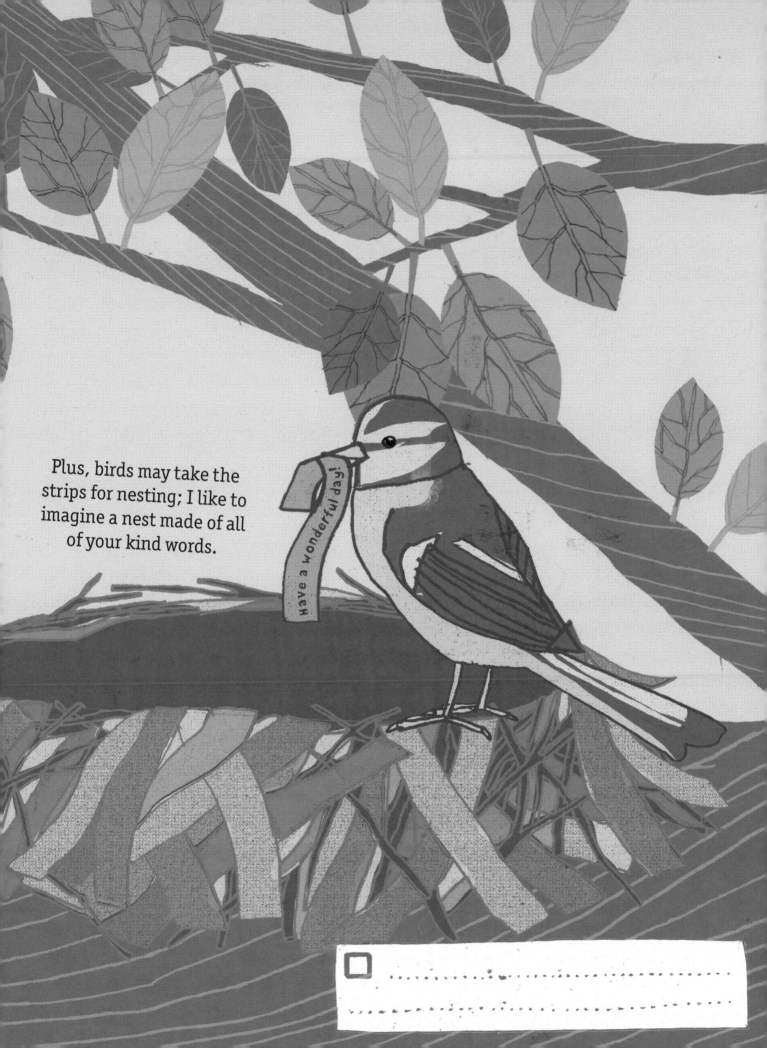

Plus, birds may take the strips for nesting; I like to imagine a nest made of all of your kind words.

Have a wonderful day!

PARKING LOT

For this one you need some scraps of paper and a car park! Be prepared - if you know it's a big one, make sure you have lots of notes. Get them ready before you go with cheerful messages like 'Have a great day!' or 'Hope you have a good journey home!'. When you get to the car park, put your notes under the windshield wipers of the parked cars - make sure the writing will be seen when the person is sitting in their car. Try to get as many cars as possible in the car park.

Once Upon A Time

Tell your mum or dad a bedtime story, like they do for you. You could read one, or make one up on the spot. This is always fun as you can make them the hero of the story.

Tip:

Silly voices are always good, as is acting out bits of the story. Make sure they are tucked up in bed and listening carefully! They might even go to sleep.

Warning: There might be snoring...

Dear Stranger

Think of something that you'd like to say to a complete stranger, and write it on a luggage label. Begin 'Dear Stranger' and end 'From [your name]'. Luggage labels are cheap to buy, and they have string so you can attach them to something if you like.

I've done this a few times and here are a few places I've tied the luggage labels:

To the handlebars of a bicycle.
On the handle of a shopping trolley
On the locker door of a changing room
On a front door handle
On the handle of a bag,

I.O.U

Make 'I Owe You A Favour' tokens for people who have been kind to you or done you a favour. Tell them they can cash in the favour whenever they like, (hopefully not all of them in one day!)

You could make your own banknotes - cut out pieces of paper the same size as a five-pound note. Then draw your own head on it, with 'One Favour' written at the bottom.

You are AWESOME because...

First, write a list of all the things that make your grandad or grandma awesome.

Take your time, as most grandparents are brilliant and there are probably more things to put on the list than you'll remember off the top of your head. Think of things they've done for you, places they've taken you, presents they've given you, and what they have done in their lives.

If you need help ask, mum or dad to tell you more about them - there might be things you don't know. Then surprise them by visiting and reading out all the things on your list.

BOX OF GOODIES

Make a 'goodie box' for one of your friends to store cool stuff in. Make your box completely out of recycled stuff (then it's kind to the environment, too!). Use an old cardboard box (shoe boxes are good) and cover it with a collage of pictures you have drawn or cut from magazines. You could put your friend's name on it by cutting letters out of old magazines, too.

YOU WILL NEED:

Scissors • Glue • An old box • Pens • Paint • Scraps of paper and old magazines for covering the box

Give it to your friend to fill with stuff they love.

OR IT!

Running a marathon is a massive task, and runners need all the support they can get. Make a sign saying 'You Are All Heroes! Run like the wind!'. Hold up your sign and shout encouragement; maybe even take down some orange segments to help quench their thirst, too!

Some runners will have their names on their vests – if you can see them, you could shout 'Go Michael/Tyler/Siobhan, you can do it!'. This will help them, especially at the tricky stage two-thirds of the way through, when everyone's legs start to ache.

Every year the marathon streaks past Kindness HQ and we shout ourselves hoarse cheering them on. One year we plan to run it, but even if that never happens we'll do our bit by encouraging and supporting the runners every year.

Extra: a lot of runners are raising money for charity; check with a charity of your choice if you can help by collecting donations on the day.

LIST OF CHORES

Make a list of chores that you could help your neighbour with, and write them down neatly on a piece of paper.

Post this note through their door, explaining that you are trying to do a kind thing every day and you would like to offer them one of the following: washing up, taking the dog for a walk, washing the car, helping in the garden.

You could write: 'This offer is valid for one month' (a good time to do this is during the school holidays). Keep a record of what happens!

HAPPY HOLIDAYS

Make a Happy Holidays card and give it to a total stranger, or pop it through the letterbox of a neighbour you don't know. The holidays are a great time of year to do this - and I'm pretty sure that the person who receives the card will be telling their family all about the wonderful surprise card they just received.

BEST
IN SHOW

Draw a picture of your neighbour's or friend's pet cat, dog, rabbit or spider (some people have very unusual pets).

Give your drawing a title like 'Best Pet in the World'. You could write beneath the picture 'This is to certify that [pet's name] has been awarded title of 'Best Pet in The World'.

Give them the picture as a present. Their cat/dog/rabbit/spider won't know they've been awarded this, of course, but it's nice for the owner to know their pet is special.

Encourage your family to have a clear
out, then make a pile of everyone's
unwanted stuff: clothes, toys, DVDs,
books and so on.

FREE STUFF

Find an old box big enough to keep everything in,
and leave the box outside your house with a sign
saying 'FREE stuff - please feel free to take me!'.

I bet it all goes pretty quickly,
and any leftovers could be taken
to your local charity shop.

☐ ....
....

TAKE CARE OF THE CARETAKER

Ask an adult for any old glass jars that are empty, then carefully wash them out. Fill the jar with candy and make a label.

Write a message on the label such as 'I hope you enjoy these treats.' Give the jar of treats to your school caretaker or cleaner to thank them for tidying up everyone's mess all year long.

Valentine's Day is a bit slushy, I admit. But in the olden days it was used as an excuse to tell anyone you liked a lot, why you liked him or her. Make a few V-day cards and send them out to people you think are great. You could compose a traditional V-day poem for each one:

'Roses are Red
Violets are Blue
I like fish and chips
And I like you, too.'

Or 'Roses are Red
Violets are Blue
I've seen your new jeans
They look good on you'

Keep it anonymous;
it'll drive them
crazy!

S.W.A.L.K

S.W.A.L.K

Bird WATCHING

Leave breadcrumbs and seeds out for hungry birds. It's good to do this in the same place every day so the birds get used to going there. It helps them all year round, especially during the chilly months.

You can leave food in your garden, on a windowsill or in the park. My sister Natalie likes to spell out 'For the birds' in breadcrumbs on her bird table, even though we're pretty sure birds can't read.

IDEA:

Make them a cake! Mix soft warm fat (such as suet or lard) into a mixture of seeds, nuts, dried fruit, oats and cheese.

Use about one-third fat to two-thirds dry mix. Stir well in a bowl and allow it to set in a container of your choice. Sing Happy Birthday to the birds when you put it outside (you don't have to do that last part, but it's fun).

A IS FOR AMAZING

Choose one of your friends who really deserves a treat. Write out your friend's name in full.

Think of a compliment beginning with each letter of their name, for example Adam could be:

Amazing

Daring

Awesome

Magical

Give them the list. You could make a name list for everyone you know, and get your friends to join in too. It's good fun to do one for a long name with unusual letters (like Zachary, Joachim or Scheherazade).

Five stars

If you have really enjoyed a book, video game, or movie, why not post a glowing online review? It will let other people know that it is great, and it's good to give positive feedback to the people who made it. Spend a bit of time considering what you most liked about it - and heap on the praise!

WRITTEN IN SAND

If you're lucky enough to get to the beach on a sunny day, write in the sand in letters as big as you can manage 'Be kind to each other: join the International Kindness Club for ninja niceness.'

This will create intrigue. Plus, if it's big enough, a passing aeroplane might see it (although it would have to be VERY big for that). No sun? No sand? No worries: you could do the same in snow in the winter. Wear gloves, so your fingers don't turn to icicles.

SOME PEOPLE ARE ANNOYING!

My old neighbour Sally had a very high voice, every time I heard her I wanted to say 'Shhhh!' Do you have someone who drives you crazy/irritates you a bit/a lot? Set yourself the challenge of being extra-double-helping nice to them. I did this and, as if by magic, Sally stopped annoying me. Now I like her voice. She's like a little bird.

Spread The Word

Here at Kindness HQ we're hoping the whole world will soon be full of members of our club. Help spread the word: you could blog about it or talk about it at school.

Imagine how awesome the world would be if every single day everyone did a kind thing!